A ROOKIE BIOGRAPHY

POCAHONTAS

Daughter of a Chief

By Carol Greene

CHILDREN'S PRESS
A Division of Grolier Publishing
Sherman Turnpike
Danbury, Connecticut 06816

This book is for Rebecca, who helped.

Pocahontas dressed as an English lady.

LIBRARY OF CONGRESS
Library of Congress Cataloging-in-Publication Data

Greene, Carol.
   Pocahontas: daughter of a chief / by Carol Greene ; Steve
Dobson, illustrator.
     p. cm. — (A Rookie biography)
   Summary: A brief biography of the American Indian
princess who as a young girl befriended John Smith, saving
him from death at the hands of her father, and later was very
helpful to the colonists at Jamestown.
   ISBN 0-516-04203-3
   1. Pocahontas, d. 1617—Juvenile literature. 2. Powhatan
Indians—Biography—Juvenile literature. 3. Smith, John, 1580-
1631—Juvenile literature. 4. Jamestown (Va.)—History—
Juvenile literature. 5. Indians of North America—Virginia—
Biography—Juvenile literature. [1. Pocahontas, d. 1617
2. Powhatan Indians—Biography. 3. Smith, John, 1580-1631.
4. Jamestown (Va.)—History. 5. Indians of North America—
Virginia—Biography.] I. Title. II. Series
E99.P85P5736   1988
[92]—dc 19
                              88-11978
                                  CIP
                                  AC

Childrens Press®, Chicago
Copyright © 1988 by Regensteiner Publishing Enterprises, Inc.
All rights reserved. Published simultaneously in Canada.
Printed in the United States of America.

10 11 12 13 14 15 16 17 18 19 R 02 01 00 99 98

Pocahontas
was a real person.
She was born around 1596.
She died in 1617.
We don't know
all about her life.
But we know she did
some brave things.
This is her story.

TABLE OF CONTENTS

The English settlers land at Jamestown, Virginia.

Chapter 1

The Strangers

Pocahontas ran through the woods.
"I must be careful," she thought.
"They must not see me.
But I must see them.
I must see the strangers."

At last the woods ended.
Pocahontas looked out
at the low, flat land.
There they were—the strangers.

"How different they look!" she thought.
"They have white skin.
They wear so many *clothes*.
Some have *hair* on their faces."

The English settlers had beards, wore armor, and carried muskets.
All of these things were strange to Pocahontas.

The colonists built wooden houses with thatch roofs.

Pocahontas watched the men work.
They cut down trees.
They built houses.
"What strange houses!"
thought Pocahontas.

Indian homes were covered with bark or reeds.

"They are not like our houses.
We bend young trees
to make the frame.
We cover the walls
with bark or reeds.
We cover the roof
with bark or grass."

Some Indian villages were surrounded by fences. John White drew this picture in 1585 after exploring in North America.

All at once, Pocahontas wanted
to meet the strangers.
"Should I?" she thought.
"Will they hurt me?"

Then she remembered.
"I am eleven years old.
My father is Chief Powhatan.
I am the daughter of a chief.
I will be brave."

So Pocahontas ran out
to meet the strangers.

Chapter 2

New Friends

Closer and closer she came.
"There are so *many* strangers,"
she thought.
"More than a hundred!"

Then she saw some boys.
They were not very old.
"Good," thought Pocahontas.
"I will meet them."

She ran to the boys.
She did not speak English.
They did not speak her language.
But soon they were playing
games together.

Who could run fastest?
Who could jump highest?
Many times Pocahontas won.

Next the boys taught her
to turn cartwheels.
"This is *fun*," thought Pocahontas.
She turned cartwheels
all over the place.

Then she had to go home.
But she came back
again and again.
Her friends taught her to say,
"Love you not me?"
They thought that was funny.
So did Pocahontas.

John Smith

She made another friend too.
He was a man
called John Smith.
He taught her more English words.
She taught him Indian words.
Sometimes he gave her beads
and other presents.

But some of the Indians
did not like the strangers.
Some of the strangers
did not like the Indians.
They were afraid of each other.

One day, some Indians
captured a white man.
They brought him
to Pocahontas' house.
It was John Smith.

This drawing of Chief Powhatan was in the book,
General History, John Smith wrote in 1607. Smith's book
told of his adventures in the Jamestown Colony.

Chief Powhatan asked him questions.

John Smith answered bravely.

Then everyone ate.

After the food,
Chief Powhatan said,
"Put two big stones
in front of me."
He made John Smith
put his head on the stones.
The Indians raised their clubs.

Then Pocahontas understood.
They were going to kill her friend!

Chapter 3

Problems

"No!" said Pocahontas.
She ran to John Smith.
She put her head
on top of his head.
"Don't kill him!" she cried.

"Stop!" said Chief Powhatan.
The men put down their clubs.
John Smith was safe.
He would go free.
Pocahontas had saved his life.

In his book, John Smith told how Pocahontas saved his life.
Many years later an artist drew this picture.

But she had done more.
She had made John Smith
a special member of the tribe.
Now he was her brother.
She was his sister.
They must help each other.

This painting shows the Jamestown Colony as it looked in 1607.

The strangers called
their town Jamestown.
One day fire broke out.
It burned their homes
and their church.
It burned their storehouse
and their food.

"Now we will starve,"
said the men of Jamestown.

"We will help you,"
said Pocahontas.
She and her friends
brought food to Jamestown.
They saved many lives.

Months went by.
The white men and Indians
traded gifts and food.
But they still did not
trust one another.

John Smith traded with the Indians.

Once Pocahontas and her friends
danced for the strangers.
They wore green leaves
and painted their bodies.
They put horns on their heads.
Out of the woods they ran.
Around the fire they danced.

"I love this dance!"
thought Pocahontas.

Indian dances were different. John White painted
this picture of an Indian dance about 1585.

But John Smith thought
it was strange.
He did not understand
Indian dances.

The English tried to give Powhatan a crown
and make him a king.

One day the strangers tried
to make Chief Powhatan a king.
They gave him a big bed,
a red coat, and a crown.

Chief Powhatan thought
that was strange.
"I don't need these things,"
he said.
"I am a great chief.
I don't need to be a king."

Now he did not like
the strangers at all.
"They are not friends," he said.
"They just want my land."

Pocahontas tried to change his mind.
But she couldn't.

"You must never go
to Jamestown again," he said.

Chapter 4

Tricks

So Pocahontas did not go
to Jamestown anymore.
But one day her father
sent for John Smith.
He promised to give John food.
But that was a trick.
He wanted to kill John.

John Smith ran away
from the chief's house.
He and his men
stayed in the woods.
Pocahontas found him there.

"Go away," she said.
"You are still in danger."

So John Smith hurried away
and Pocahontas hurried home.
"My father must not find out
that I helped John," she thought.
"He might kill *me*.
But I had to help John.
He is my brother."

The new colonists did not like the way
John Smith ran Jamestown.

Back at Jamestown,
John Smith found more trouble.
Many new English people had come.
They needed food.
They didn't like John Smith.
They wanted a new leader.

Then John got burned
in a fire.
"I will go to England
and rest a while," he thought.
"Then I will come back here."

"Where is John Smith?"
asked the Indians.

The white men lied.
"He is dead," they said.

When Pocahontas heard that,
she felt very sad.

Powhatan's men attacked the Jamestown colonists.

But the other Indians were glad.
They began to fight
the people at Jamestown.
Pocahontas hated the fighting.
But she couldn't stop it.

So she went away.
She stayed with Indian friends
for almost four years.

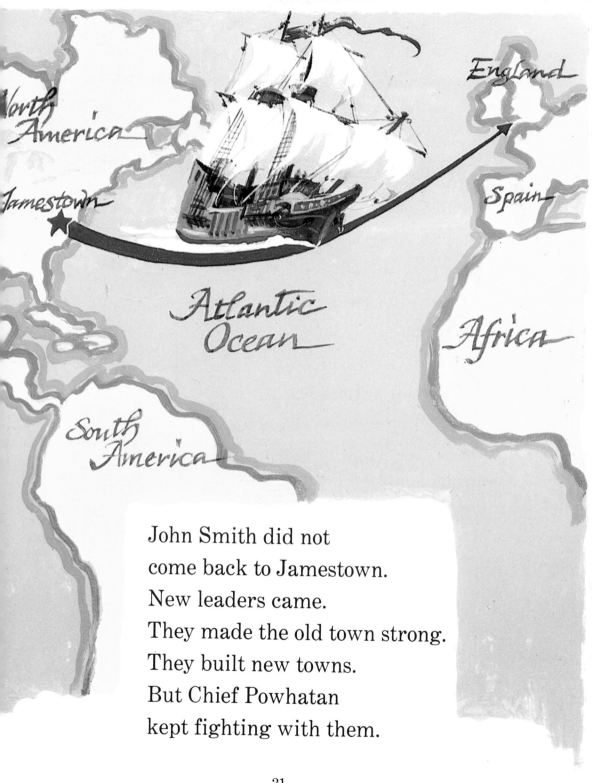

John Smith did not
come back to Jamestown.
New leaders came.
They made the old town strong.
They built new towns.
But Chief Powhatan
kept fighting with them.

"We must stop Powhatan,"
said the people of Jamestown.

Then Captain Samuel Argall
talked to Pocahontas' friends.
If they would trick her,
he would give them a copper kettle.

"All right," said the friends.
They wanted that kettle.

Pocahontas was tricked into getting on Captain Argall's ship.

"Let's go see an English ship,"
they said to Pocahontas.
She didn't want to.
But she went.

They ate with Captain Argall
on the ship.
Then the friends sneaked away.
They left Pocahontas.
She was a prisoner!

Chapter 5

A New Way of Life

The ship sailed to Jamestown.
"You must make peace
with the English people,"
Captain Argall told Chief Powhatan.
"Then Pocahontas can go free."

But the chief did nothing.
The white men sent Pocahontas
to stay with a minister.
He taught her about God.
She met the women
in his church.
They taught her to dress
like an English lady.

About 1905 Richard N. Brooke, an artist, painted Pocahontas dressed as an English lady.

Pocahontas was baptized and given the new name Rebecca.

At last Pocahontas said
she wanted to be a Christian.
She was given
a new name—Rebecca.

She met a kind man, too.
His name was John Rolfe.
John Rolfe and Pocahontas
fell in love.
They wanted to get married.

Then Chief Powhatan said
he would make peace.
Pocahontas was glad.
But she did not want
to go home anymore.

In 1614 Pocahontas married John Rolfe. Hundreds of years later, an artist painted this picture. Do you think that Pocahontas really looked like this picture?

She and John were married.
A year later, they had a baby.
They called him Thomas.

Pocahontas and her son Thomas Rolfe

One day leaders
came to Pocahontas.
"We want you to go to England,"
they said.
"Other English people will see you.
They will like you
and want to come here."

In 1616 Pocahontas went to live in London, England.

So Pocahontas got on a ship
and went to England.
John and Thomas went too.
She met many English people.
She even met the king and queen.

King James I was the ruler of England, Scotland, and the Virginia Colony when Pocahontas met him.

Then someone told Pocahontas
that John Smith was alive.
He was living in England.

"Why doesn't he come see me?"
she asked.
"He is my *brother*."

41

She waited almost a year.
Then John Smith came.
Pocahontas was happy.
At first she could not even talk.
How good it was
to see her brother again!

After a while, the damp weather
in England made Pocahontas sick.
She knew she was going to die.
But Pocahontas was not afraid.
She was still the brave
daughter of a chief.

Pocahontas was buried
in a church at Gravesend, England.
Many people still visit her grave.
They will not forget
the brave Indian girl
who wanted the English people
and Indians to be friends.

Pocahontas

1596? Born to Chief Powhatan

1607 First visited Jamestown
      Saved John Smith's life

1608 Took food to Jamestown

1609 Saved John Smith's life again

1610 Visited Indian friends

1613 Made a prisoner on
      Captain Argall's ship

1614 Married to John Rolfe

1615 Son Thomas born

1616 Went to England

1617 Died at Gravesend, England

INDEX

Page numbers in boldface type indicate illustrations.

PHOTO CREDITS

ABOUT THE AUTHOR

Carol Greene has degrees in English Literature and Musicology. She has
worked in international exchange programs, as an editor, and as a teacher. She
now lives in St. Louis, Missouri, and writes full time. She has published over
seventy books, most of them for children. Other Childrens Press biographies by
Ms. Greene include *Louisa May Alcott, Marie Curie, Thomas Alva Edison,
Hans Christian Andersen, Marco Polo,* and *Wolfgang Amadeus Mozart* in the
People of Distinction series, *Sandra Day O'Connor, Mother Teresa, Indira
Nehru Gandhi, Diana, Princess of Wales, Desmond Tutu,* and *Elie Wiesel* in the
Picture-Story Biography series, and *Pocahontas* and *Benjamin Franklin* in the
Rookie Biography series.